C0-BIJ-861

Conceived and produced by
Lionheart Books
10 Chelmsford Square
London NW10 3AR

Editor Lionel Bender,
assisted by Madeleine Samuel
Designer Ben White

From an original idea by
Lionel Bender and Dr. J. F. Oates,
Primatologist, Hunter College,
New York

Copyright © Lionheart Books 1987

Adapted and published in
the United States
by Silver Burdett Press,
Morristown, New Jersey.

*Library of Congress Cataloging in
Publication Data*

Stidworthy, John, 1943–
    Whale.

    (A Year in the life)
    Includes index.
    Summary: Describes a year in the life
of male sperm whale who lives most of
the time in cold Arctic waters, except for
the time he goes south to tropical waters
to mate.
    1. Sperm whale–Juvenile literature.
(1. Sperm whale. 2. Whales)
I. Colville, Jeane, ill.   II. Title
III. Series: Stidworthy, John, 1943–
Year in the life.
QL737.C435S75   1987   599.5'3
86-31427
ISBN 0-382-09446-8
ISBN 0-382-09455-7 (pbk.)

A YEAR IN THE LIFE: WHALE
Written by John Stidworthy
Illustrated by Jeane Colville

ABOUT THIS BOOK

Our book tells the story of the life of one particular whale over a single year. We have written and illustrated our story as if we had watched the whale's behavior through the year, noticing how its activities changed at different periods. By looking closely at one whale, we give you a good understanding of how an individual animal reacts to others and to the conditions it experiences in the wild.

We have called our whale Kaska. On pages 4 and 5 we show you where Kaska lives and tell you a little about Kaska's habits and lifestyle. Our main story, on pages 6 to 29, follows a year in Kaska's life, and is divided up into six sections between one and three months long. Each section begins with a large illustration showing the environment and one aspect of Kaska's behavior at that time. The following two pages in each section continue our main story and show some of Kaska's other activities during the same period. On page 30 we discuss whale conservation.

Whales are mammals and as such breathe air using lungs and give birth to live young, which the mother feeds on her milk. Over millions of years whales have become adapted to living in the sea. They are streamlined for swimming, and have tail flukes to push against the water. Hind legs have disappeared and front legs have turned to flippers for steering. The nostrils have moved away from the mouth so that whales breathe and smell through a blowhole on top of the head.

There are two main types of whale. The baleen whales have horny plates in their mouth to sieve small food items from the water. The toothed whales do not sieve water, but catch big prey such as fish and squid. They have from 2 to 200 pointed teeth. There are nearly 70 kinds of toothed whale, ranging from small dolphins and porpoises up to killer whales and the largest, the subject of this book, the sperm whale, scientific name *Physeter macrocephalus*.

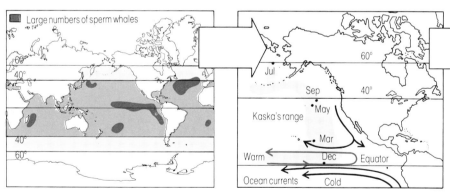

△ Sperm whales are found almost worldwide. Males range from the equator nearly to the poles. Females and young rarely go beyond 40°N or 40°S. The whales rarely cross the equator.

△ Sperm whales seem most common in areas where there are strong ocean currents flowing against one another, and also close to the deep ocean trenches where food is plentiful.

Our sperm whale, Kaska

Kaska is a young adult male about 25 years old. Sperm whales can live 50 years. Males, called bulls, grow larger than females, which are known as cows. Young sperm whales are called calves. We meet Kaska in July when he is at the north of his range.

Whales are difficult to observe. The little we know about them – what they look like, where they are easiest to find, what they eat – is based mostly on chance sightings.

The seasons

In the course of a year sperm whales make long migrations. In autumn they swim towards the equator and in spring towards the poles. Males travel much farther than the females. Females live in groups all year round and rarely leave warm waters. Males are solitary in high summer, but most join up with female groups in winter and spring. The breeding season is quite long, but the peak time for births is late summer.

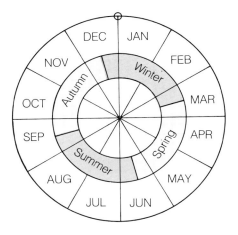

△ The calendar in Kaska's range. A small calendar is used in the book to show the time span of each section.

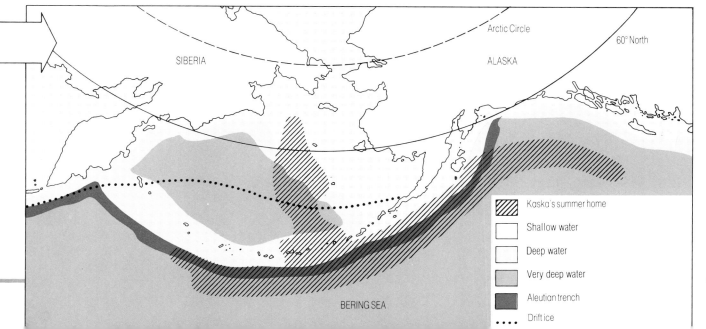

5

Kaska was resting at the surface of the sea. He had come up from a deep dive with a stomach full of food and had taken several deep breaths. Now he was breathing more gently and swimming slowly. He was in the middle of the Bering Sea between Alaska and the Soviet Union, at about 60°N. Even now, in the middle of the summer, there were some floating patches of ice. But Kaska did not feel cold. The thick layer of fatty blubber under his skin insulated him from the cold water.

As a young adult, Kaska was still growing but was already nearly fifty feet long and weighed nearly thirty tons. Yet his huge size did not bother him. The water supported his body and he could float at the surface without effort. As he swam, he used the big muscles along his back to lift his tail and allow his wide

tail flukes to push against the water.

Kaska dipped his head into the water and swam just below the surface. As he went he produced a series of deep click sounds which were beamed out from his head into the water. He could hear the echoes of these clicks bouncing back from objects in the water. The echoes told him much of what he knew about the outside world. Kaska also heard some other very faint clicks, the voice of another sperm whale several miles away.

Kaska was swimming north, but now echoes from the sea floor told him the sea ahead was shallow. He headed first east, then west, but the sea floor loomed closer. Kaska preferred deep water. He turned and began swimming south again, towards the chain of Aleutian Islands that he had passed two weeks before.

7

Aware of his surroundings

Kaska lifted his head out of the water, his attention caught by a flock of birds. He could see quite well but underwater he often dived down into total darkness where eyes were not an important sense. For most of the time he kept his blowhole closed so he could smell nothing, but using his tongue he could taste substances in the water. Kaska relied on his hearing to guide him.

△ The eyes of a sperm whale are set at the sides of the head. The whale can probably see everywhere except directly ahead. Small ear openings are set behind the eyes.

Blowing

As he traveled, Kaska kept diving and coming up for air. Each time he surfaced he opened the blowhole at the tip of his nose, blew out used air, then took a fast deep breath. This way he rapidly renewed the air in his lungs.

▷ A whale's spout consists of air from its lungs, water vapor, and foam from its air passages. The sperm whale's spout shoots forward, from the blowhole on the top left of its head.

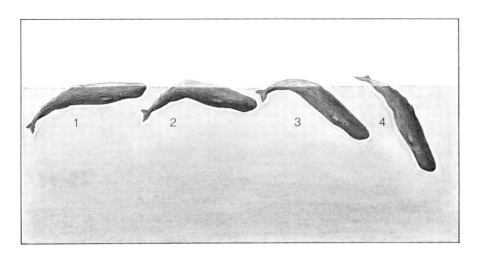

Diving deep

Kaska was ready to dive again. He forced up his tail against the water and bent his body so his head pointed down. He went down almost vertically and, as his body straightened out, his flukes appeared above the water. He swam steadily downward until he was in the dark, cold waters hundreds of feet below. Here he leveled out and swam slowly, searching for prey. He stopped in the water and listened. Today in the sea there were few other animals. The only echoes he heard were from icebergs far in the distance. He moved on.

For half an hour he stayed submerged. Then his body began to signal that its supply of oxygen was running low. Just as deliberately as he had gone down he began to swim up again. He burst to the surface, and with one huge breath that lasted three seconds he almost emptied his lungs of stale air. A second later he had filled them again. After thirty such breaths he was ready to dive once more.

▷ Whales store oxygen in their muscles and on a dive use this and the oxygen in their lungs to stay alive. When they surface, they breathe repeatedly until they have replaced the oxygen used.

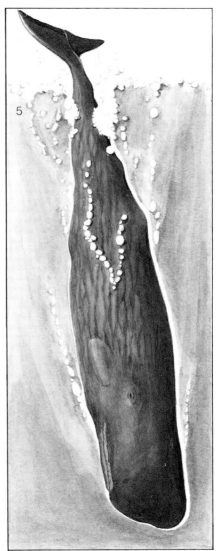

For a few weeks Kaska stayed in the seas just south of the Aleutian Islands, one of the deepest parts of the ocean. But as the short Arctic summer drew to a close he began to swim southward. Most of the time he was moving parallel to the west coast of Canada and the United States, but he kept well out to sea in the deep ocean. As he traveled, Kaska came across other mature males also returning from northern waters. Occasionally they swam together for a while, but most of the time Kaska journeyed alone, although he often heard the voices of other males in the distance. The larger the whale the fewer clicks it made each minute, so from the sounds Kaska could judge each whale's size. Sometimes he recognized an individual he had met before. Off Vancouver, widely spaced clicks told Kaska he was passing a sperm whale almost one-and-a-half times his length and nearly twice as heavy!

Some 700 miles farther south, Kaska started to meet groups of female sperm whales and their young. He felt eager for the company of females. Off San Francisco he passed a group he had met a year before, and recognized their voices. But a mature bull was with them, so Kaska moved on. He found many groups of females, but most had one or two adult bulls swimming with them. At last, when he had reached warm tropical seas, Kaska met a group that contained some females he knew and some youngsters but had no attendant adult male. Kaska began to swim close to the group's flank.

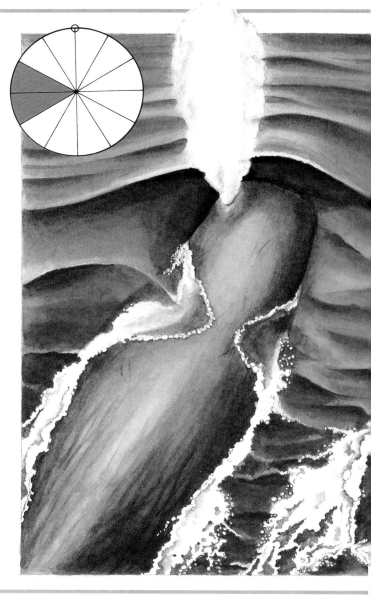

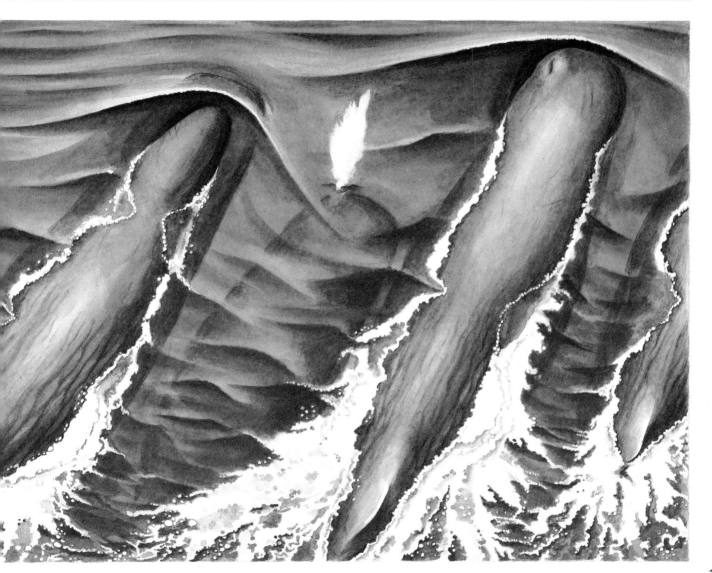

Social life

Kaska's group contained seven mature cows. The largest was shorter and much slimmer than Kaska. Three of the cows each had a calf with them that had been born that year. The other nine animals in the group (pod) were immature males and females of various ages.

▷ A "pod" of sperm whales is up to 20 strong and consists of females and young. Adult males mostly live alone and join a pod only for breeding.

A new life

Soon after Kaska's arrival another female in the group gave birth. The other females noticed the mother's movements and gathered close to her to comfort her. The baby's tail appeared first. For a minute or two only the flukes showed outside the mother, then, quite quickly, the rest of the little whale emerged. Immediately the calf tried to swim and the adults moved to it and helped lift it to the air to take its first breath.

▷ A newborn sperm whale measures some 12 feet long and weighs about a ton. It must quickly get to the surface to fill its lungs with air.

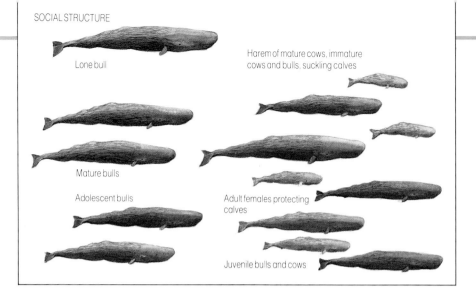

SOCIAL STRUCTURE

Lone bull

Harem of mature cows, immature cows and bulls, suckling calves

Mature bulls

Adolescent bulls

Adult females protecting calves

Juvenile bulls and cows

Birth begins

Taking care

The little whale was soon able to swim alongside its mother. The water flowed around the big whale in a way that made it easy for the baby to swim, even though its swimming strokes were not yet very powerful.

Kaska took little notice of the new arrival, but by being around he made life safer for the group. Few creatures would attack an adult male sperm whale. Kaska could watch and chase away any animal approaching too close. Most creatures Kaska met were harmless. Sometimes he lifted his head to watch the lively jumping of passing groups, or schools, of dolphins. There were many of these to be seen as Kaska's group kept on the move through the seas towards the equator. The whales seemed to stop only to sleep.

▽ A sperm whale baby grows inside its mother's body for 16 months until birth. The newborn feeds on milk from its mother. It suckles for a little over a year.

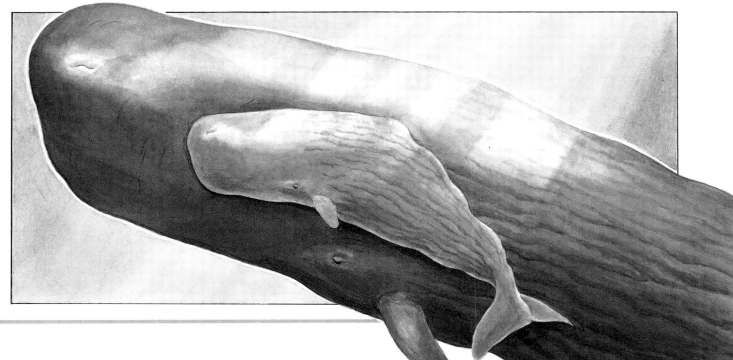

By December Kaska and his group were almost on the equator near the Galapagos Islands. Here warm ocean currents met colder currents moving up from deep seas off the west coast of South America. The cold currents brought plenty of food for the equatorial ocean life. The sperm whales fed on fish and, especially, on squid. On a good hunting day Kaska might capture as much as a ton of squid. When he was hunting he sometimes went right down to the ocean bottom more than one mile below. Occasionally he swam slowly along the bottom dropping his lower jaw to plow the mud for food. More often, though, he stayed almost still, deep in the water, waiting in ambush for shoals of squid.

One day Kaska was waiting for prey when he sensed a large animal approaching fast. Echoes had told him squid were around, but not until this one was within reach and he had snapped his narrow jaw shut on it did he realize how big it was. Most squid just disappeared into Kaska's open mouth, but this one fought back. Its tentacles writhed, and Kaska felt their suckers fasten onto his skin. The squid snapped its beak and nearly bit him. Kaska bit again and crushed the animal in his jaws. Gradually the squid lost its strength and Kaska was able to swallow it, but he bore the marks of the struggle for a long time afterwards.

From the tip of its tentacles to the end of its body, this giant squid was nearly as long as Kaska and was the biggest he had ever met.

15

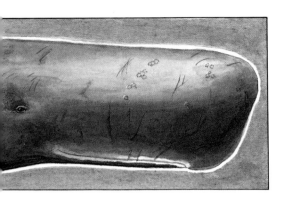

△ The pattern of scars on a whale's head is as distinctive as a signature. The huge nose bears a sac full of liquid wax that surrounds the nasal passages.

Battle scars and weapons

Kaska's head now had fresh sucker wounds in addition to earlier scars. It also bore marks left by sperm whale teeth. These were mostly scratches from wrestling with other young males as he grew up, but also a set of puncture marks where a bad-tempered old bull had attacked him. Few male sperm whales were without a set of scars but cows were much less marked.

The sharp pointed teeth in Kaska's lower jaw fitted into sockets in his upper jaw. He used his teeth to help capture large prey. Kaska's teeth, like those of other sperm whales, had not emerged from his gums until he was ten years old, well after he began catching prey for himself. More important perhaps for Kaska was that he could use his teeth as weapons against enemies and rivals. At present, though, there were no threats. He and the females, his "harem," could spend their time peacefully diving for squid in the food-rich waters.

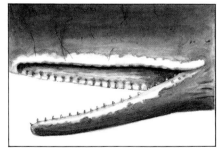

◁ Sperm whales feed on squid of all sizes. Many squid have light-emitting organs that may make them visible in the deep, but the whales are thought to hunt mainly by sound. The typical size of squid eaten is about 3 feet long but one whale stomach contained 28,000 squid, mainly much smaller. Sperm whales also eat fish, including sharks and rays.

Within the group, the larger whales were able to stay under water longest. When the group was busy traveling, however, individuals rarely made their maximum length dives and often surfaced, breathed, and dived together. Each seemed to sense what the others were about to do.

To feed their calves, the mothers paused on the surface and turned on their sides. Their two teats stuck out from the body fold in which they were usually hidden. Each calf took a teat in its mouth and its mother pumped milk into it. The whole process was quickly over and scarcely slowed the progress of the group in the water.

Surfacing from the abyss

Kaska dived deeper than any of the females or young whales. At times he stayed down for almost an hour. After a long deep dive he would surface fast, sometimes shooting right out through the surface of the water and falling back again with a tremendous splash. He was unable to make another long dive until he had fully recharged his oxygen store, which could require forty deep breaths. Occasionally, though, he would take no more than ten short breaths and dive for just a minute or two.

△ In a deep dive a whale experiences enormous pressures but suffers no harm from this or the rapid dive and ascent.

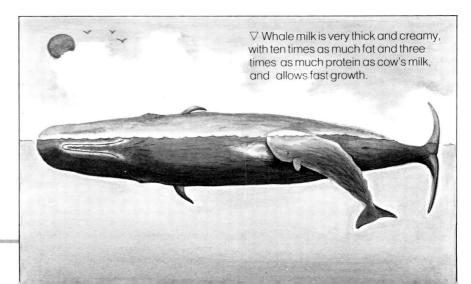

▽ Whale milk is very thick and creamy, with ten times as much fat and three times as much protein as cow's milk, and allows fast growth.

RIVALRY ON THE HIGH SEAS

Kaska and the group stayed in the tropics as the New Year arrived. They were finding plenty to eat, and although they kept slowly on the move they seemed to have no particular goal as they wandered the seas west of the Galapagos Islands. There seemed to be nothing to interrupt their peaceful life of leisurely swimming and diving. One morning an adult bull whale appeared, swimming on a course leading to the group. Kaska felt the newcomer to be a threat. He changed his own course slightly to head off the other whale. He rose out of the water and the two animals stared at each other. Then, still at the surface, Kaska quickened his speed and launched an attack. The newcomer realized he was coming and turned to face him. As the two whales collided, Kaska rolled over and snapped his jaw, trying to catch the other bull's jaw in his own. The sea was whipped into a mass of foam as the two huge bodies twisted and wrestled. They swam apart then rushed at each other again. Both were cut and bleeding where sharp teeth had gouged pieces of flesh. The struggle continued for some minutes, then the newcomer turned away. Kaska did not pursue him.

Both whales were injured, with deep scratches and holes in their skin and in some places with torn flesh and blubber, and both had broken teeth. Kaska had won the battle by determination rather than greater strength. Sore but still feeling strong, he returned to the group of females for which he had fought.

Hangers-on

The wounds Kaska had received in his struggle with the bull whale irritated him but there was nothing he could do about them. The sea water cleansed them, however, and in time they would heal. Kaska could do nothing too about the animals that lived on his skin. He could not scratch himself. Always there were whale lice, little shelled animals that lived in every wrinkle and crevice of his skin. They thrived in his wounds. He could also feel the barnacles and remoras that clung to him. These did not harm Kaska or compete with him for food but used him only to get around.

Stalked barnacles

△ Whales are often hosts to stalked barnacles similar to those found on ships' bottoms. The barnacles mark the skin on the flukes and lips, where they most often grow, but feed from the water.

▽ Whales in warm seas may have remoras attached. These fish use sucker pads on their heads to hitch a ride. They repay their carriers by feeding on the little animals on their skins.

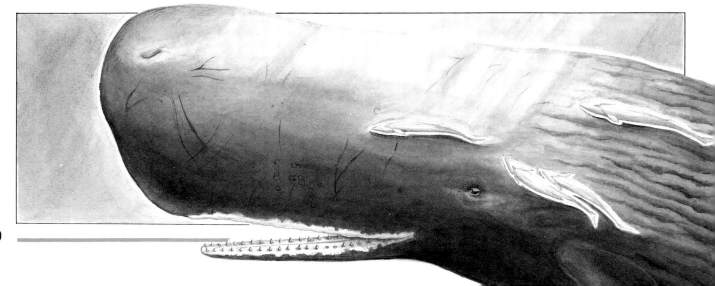

Fending off attackers

For some days after his fight Kaska's jaw felt stiff. When he dived and caught squid the movement opened up one of his wounds and made him bleed again. Before long sharks arrived, attracted by the scent of blood. Kaska ignored them as they swam past. But then they turned and followed him. He did not like being shadowed by large creatures not of his own kind. Annoyed, he lashed out with his tail flukes, slapping them at the sharks. The sudden blows frightened the sharks and they scattered at high speed. They did not return.

Kaska felt the need to be on the move. He gradually began to swim north, and his harem followed. Although it was far from a steady progress, by the last weeks of February the group had moved away from the equator and were over 900 miles out to sea off the coast of southern Mexico. As they journeyed, the seas did not always provide good hunting, but the whales felt restless and wanted to move on. They had fed well for some time and had plenty of fat reserves in their blubber. The calves that had been born last year had all survived and were growing fast and well.

△ Even large sharks are unlikely to be a threat to an adult whale unless it is badly injured. Sperm whales defend themselves using their jaws and teeth, by hitting with their tails, or sometimes by ramming attackers with their heads

MATING TIME

As springtime in the north approached, the whales were swimming more determinedly than ever. They were clearly making a northward migration. They swam steadily in the same direction for days at a time, slowing only to dive for food. As well as Kaska's group, many other sperm whales were making the same journey. On some days, so many whales were moving together that the whole sea, from horizon to horizon, seemed full of whales rising to breathe. Yet the groups did not really mingle.

Out to sea off northern Mexico the pace of the migration slowed. Kaska's group swam away from the main migration route and remained in one part of the ocean. Here the water was cooler than farther south but it was not cold enough to trouble the calves, which had thinner coats of blubber than the adults. There was food enough for all the whales. Kaska, though, was not especially interested in food. It was the sperm whales' mating season and he set about courting the females. He followed the largest female and swam alongside her. She moved away swimming fast, but he pursued her and came alongside again. He rubbed his body against hers. For an hour they swam together, repeatedly touching and moving apart. Kaska clasped her jaw gently in his. Then he let go and they touched again. Finally they rose a little out of the water and they mated quickly before sliding back into the sea with a splash.

Kaska did not stay long with this female. Soon he began the same courtship chase with another one. Before the mating season was over, Kaska had mated with all five females in the group that were ready to mate. Three of these were mature females that had borne calves before. The other two were young females, only ten years old, that were mating for the first time. All the rest of the females in the group were either too young to breed or already had a calf they were suckling. It would be two years before these would breed again. Kaska was breeding for the first time, but he could expect many more years in which he could win and mate with a group of females.

Giant at play

During the weeks in the breeding area Kaska fed well and was energetic. When he was not pursuing the females or feeding, he did things that appeared to be sheer fun and adventure, perhaps to attract the females to him. Sometimes he dived a little then shot to the surface, pushing his body into the air before falling

◁ Most adult animals do not "play" but a sperm whale's acrobatics seem to be exactly this. "Playfulness" often goes with intelligence. Sperm whales have the biggest brain of any animal.

sideways with a thunderous crash. Occasionally he jumped so high he left the water completely. As he tumbled back, the sound of his huge body breaking the surface of the water could be heard by every whale for miles around. Another game he played was to stand on his head with his tail out of the water, slapping the flukes one way then the other.

▽ Actions such as breaching (jumping from the water) and lobtailing (slapping the water with the flukes) make lots of noise and may serve to attract female whales or repel possible male rivals.

Protecting the young

Life was not all carefree. One day while he was diving Kaska heard alarm calls being given by the females swimming above. He headed up to the surface as fast as he could. He could hear some unfamiliar clicks and splashing a little way off. Lifting his head from the water, he saw a school of six killer whales. Some of these were upright in the water looking towards him, others were swimming menacingly close. The female sperm whales clumped together, their heads facing outwards, to form a defensive circle around the calves. A killer whale is little match for an adult sperm whale, but a lone calf would be easy prey and Kaska realized this.

Kaska clapped his jaw angrily and charged at full speed towards the killer whales. For a moment it looked as though a fight would occur, but then the six smaller whales turned tail and swam off to look for easier prey. After a while Kaska and his group felt safe enough to resume diving.

▽ Sperm whales, particularly females, take great care of other members of their group. They help others in distress or injured, and may support them in the water so they can breathe easily.

ALONE AGAIN

By early summer all mating behavior in Kaska's group had ended. The whales had moved a little farther north into the seas between San Francisco and Hawaii. Most of the group were content in these warm waters, but Kaska felt restless again. He began to swim greater distances each day. To begin with he circled around and came back to the group, but he had lost interest in the females and gradually swam farther away until he lost touch with them. Kaska then began to swim northward. Soon he was farther north than the females and young ever ventured.

Other lone males, and young males traveling together in groups, were swimming north too. Kaska remained alone, pleasing himself where he went and how fast he traveled. With no need to keep in step with other whales, he would dive deep and stay down for long periods. He explored and tested unfamiliar objects to see if they were edible. He nibbled at a telephone cable on the sea bed but rejected it. Then he plucked a huge skate from the muddy bottom.

Kaska was not hurrying, but when he was swimming he kept up a steady speed of four miles an hour. By June he had reached the cold waters near the Aleutian Islands where he had been almost a year before. He dived and explored the deep water there, just as happy to be alone again as a few months before he had been comfortable in the company of a group of sperm whales. Kaska fed well. He had grown noticeably in the last year.

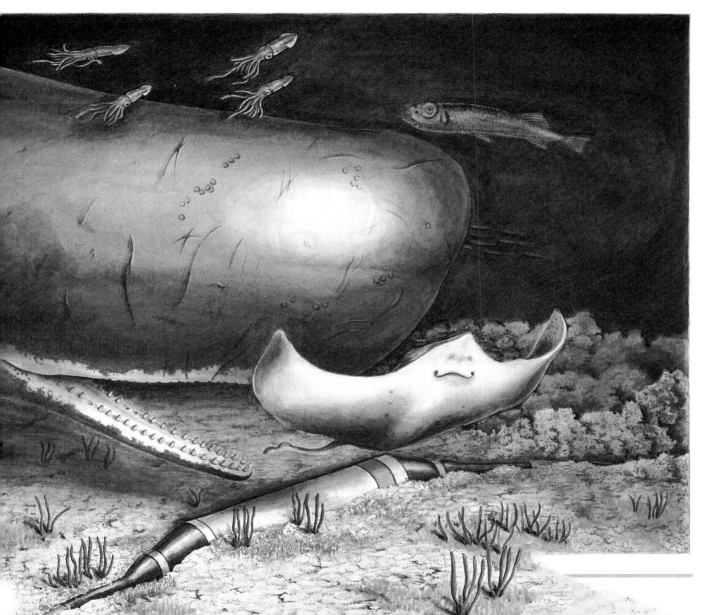

Alarm

Going north, Kaska had experienced one moment of alarm. It was a day when many whales were in the same area. A small ship appeared. The noise of its engines alerted the whales but the schools of young males and the older loners like Kaska kept swimming steadily. The ship was a research vessel charting the sea and investigating marine life. Scientists on board had come to look at and

count the large concentration of migrating whales. The ship came close to Kaska. At first he sensed no danger but then the engine sounds became very loud and he dived. He came up again cautiously. The vessel was now quieter, its engines shut right down. Then the engines started again with a roar. Kaska took fright and swam away speedily until he was well clear of the ship and felt safe. The ship did not pursue him.

◁△ Sperm whales can be approached closely by a boat if this is done quietly, but will be alarmed by sudden or strange sounds. The whales escape by diving or fast swimming.

Return to the north

Kaska had reached the end of his migration. He dived in the deep cold waters of the Aleutian trench and explored the sea bottom until he knew the area well. Then he swam farther west and explored. Some of the sperm whales he heard here had unfamiliar voices. They had migrated north from the west side of the Pacific. For many generations their ancestors and Kaska's had followed different migration routes. A little farther north, but far from the mainland, were islands dotted with colonies of seabirds and sealions. Kaska was sometimes surrounded by these animals diving for food. However, he could dive deeper than any of them and find food they could not reach.

Kaska would be growing for several seasons more and, with luck, would live to repeat his annual migrations for at least another twenty years.

▷ In the N. Hemisphere the distance between a male sperm whale's summer and winter home is about 5,000 miles. Females and young make annual N-S movements but do not go farther north than about 40°N.

The sperm whale has been hunted commercially since the 18th century. With faster whaling boats and factory ships, attention turned to other great whales like the blue whale in the Antarctic, but as these were killed off the sperm whale once again became the hunters' chief target. The annual catch reached 30,000 in 1963. Since then, decline in numbers, setting of lower permitted catches and finally in 1979 the banning of factory-ship whaling, have cut the catch of sperm whales noticeably. Some are still caught by "traditional" whaling methods or by pirate whalers, but for the time being they are not in danger of being hunted to extinction.

Besides the oil that can be boiled out of its blubber, and its meat, the sperm whale has been in demand because of the spermaceti wax from its enormous nose. The oil from this makes smokeless candles and lamps, and is considered important for lubricating delicate machinery. However, it is now possible to extract an almost identical oil from a desert plant, the jojoba, and there is no need to kill sperm whales.

There is no accurate knowledge of how many sperm whales there are in the world. Some of the most likely guesses put the number at about half a million. We do know there are not so many as there once were, and while the sperm whale is easily the most numerous of the big whales, being spread over all the oceans of the world it is common in only a few places. The seas around South Africa contain the largest population.

For more information
Useful information about whale conservation can be obtained from the World Wildlife Fund,
1601 Connecticut Ave. N.W.,
Washington, D.C. 20009 and from
Save the Whales, P.O. Box 3650,
Washington, D.C. 20007.

▷ The sperm whale industry still exists in Iceland, South Africa, and the Azores in the mid-Atlantic.

Photo: Tony Martin/Oxford Scientific Films

Fact file

The diagram alongside shows the year's main events for Kaska and his group of females and young. In other parts of the world the events tend to occur in different months. There seems to be a connection between seasonal changes in ocean currents and weather and the sperm whale's behavior, but we do not fully understand this.

	JUL	AUG	SEP	OCT	NOV	DEC	JAN	FEB	MAR	APR	MAY	JUN
Kaska	Northernmost	Aleutians	Moving south		In tropics	Galapagos			Moving north	Breeding grounds	Moving north	
Females and calves	Male and Female live apart					Male and Female live together					M and F apart	
	Cruising 30°–40°N				Going south	In tropics	Galapagos		Moving north	Breeding grounds	Remain in same general area	
			Main birth season			Kaska's breeding season						